GW01167911

BBC SPARK ISLAND

INTERACTIVE LEARNING ADVENTURES

Notes for Parents

This book has been created, written and designed by teachers and educationalists to support the development of core English skills linked to the National Curriculum and Scottish Guidelines.

Remember these three key points when you and your child are working:

a) Always pick a quiet time and make sure you have the time to help if your child needs it.

b) Offer help when your child asks for it; don't rush in with advice.

c) Talk about the activities your child likes and why they like them.

How this book works

1 Learning

This section will give you examples and instructions to help you to make the most of this book.

2 Practice

This area allows your child to complete an activity and practise their skills. Where possible we have completed the first questions, which will give your child another clue to help them to complete the activity.

3 Parents' Notes

These notes are designed to help you as a parent to support your child. It might be a gentle hint or a more general comment about what your child is learning.

Using the CD-ROM and Website

The Spark Island CD-ROM that comes with this book provides three practice activities to do on your computer as well as a bank of activity sheets that you can print out and complete with your child. We recommend using the CD-ROM after each page with the CD symbol on it. However, this is just a guide and using the activities on the computer at any time will help your child to practise the important skills.

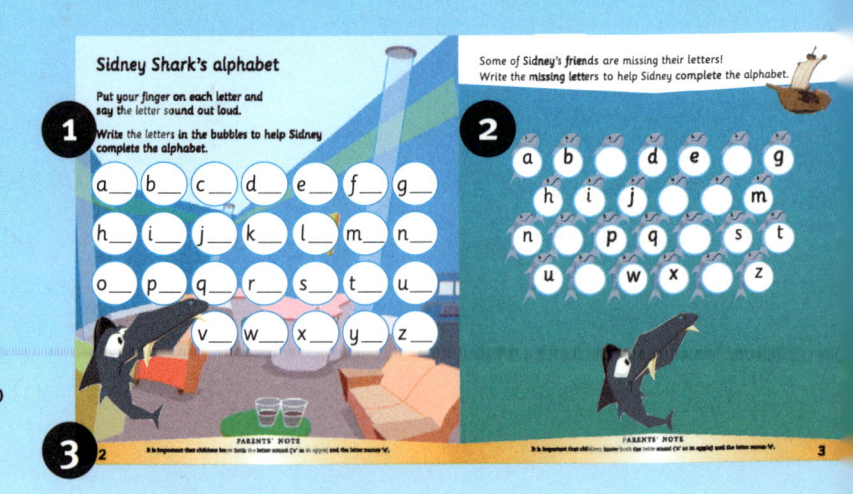

Our website at http://www.sparkisland.com contains a wealth of activities and lots more parents' notes. The website is used in schools throughout the UK and has been tested by teachers, so you can be confident that it provides educationally sound and relevant activities to improve your child's skills.

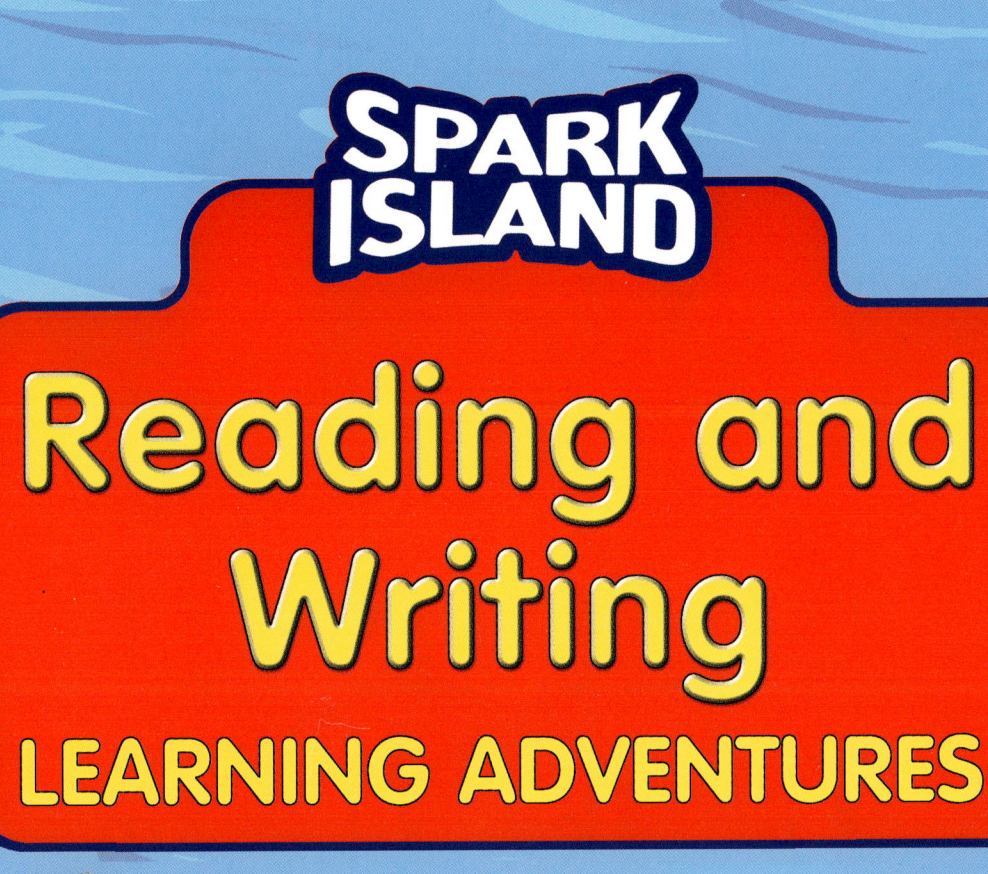

Spark Island

Reading and Writing
LEARNING ADVENTURES

For Ages 5-7 ENGLISH

BBC

Sidney the Shark's alphabet

Put your finger on each letter and say the letter sound out loud.

Write the letters in the bubbles to help Sidney complete the alphabet.

a__ b__ c__ d__ e__ f__ g__

h__ i__ j__ k__ l__ m__ n__

o__ p__ q__ r__ s__ t__ u__

v__ w__ x__ y__ z__

PARENTS' NOTE
It is important that children know both the letter sound ('a' as in apple) and the letter name 'a'.

Some of Sidney's friends are missing their letters!
Write the missing letters to help Sidney complete the alphabet.

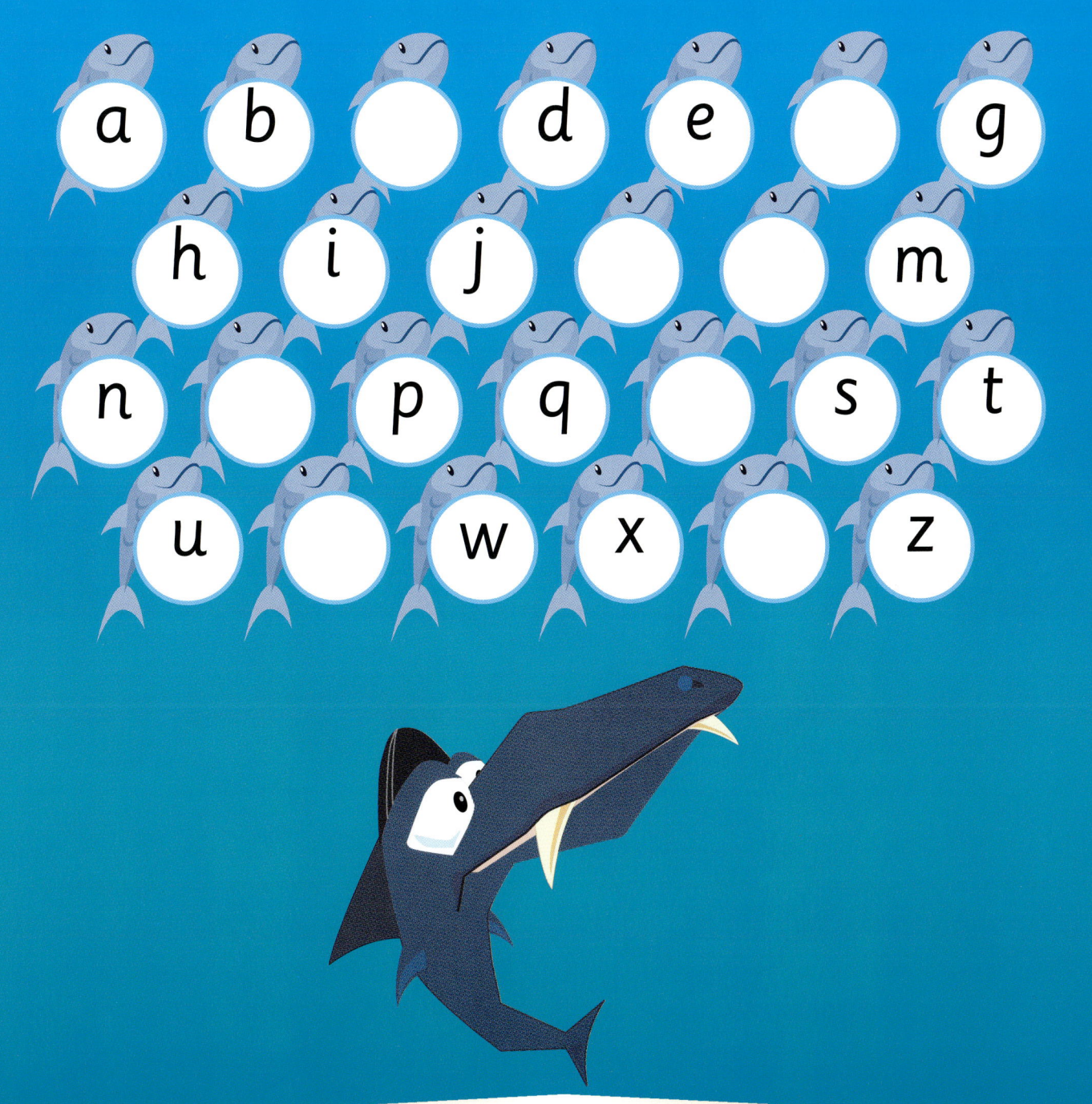

a b _ d e _ g
h i j _ _ m
n _ p q _ s t
u _ w x _ z

PARENTS' NOTE
It is important that children know both the letter sound ('a' as in apple) and the letter name 'a'.

Complete Norman's words: first letters

Norman has lost the first letters in his words!
Can you help him to complete the words?
Write the missing first letter to finish each word.
Then write the whole word under the picture.

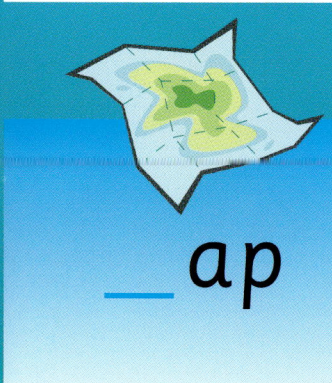

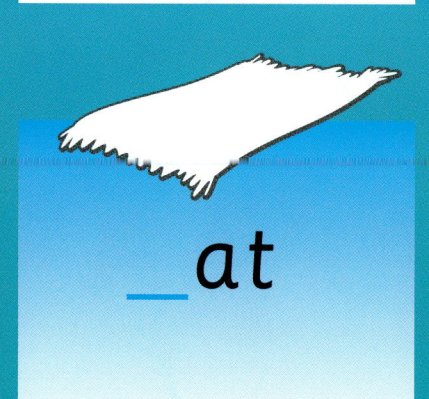

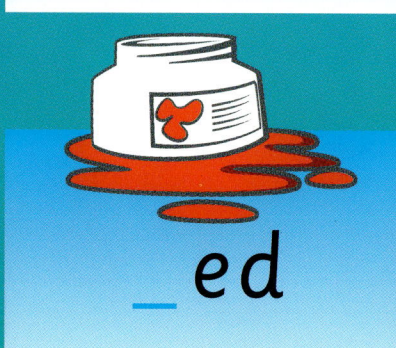

bag
bag

_at

_un

_ap

_at

_an

_ug

_at

_ed

PARENTS' NOTE
These words are all simple CVC (or consonant, vowel, consonant) words. They use common short letter sounds.

Norman is still missing some letters.
Can you help him to find them?

cap
cap

_at

_an

_at

_ut

_en

_en

_an

_ig

PARENTS' NOTE
These words are all simple CVC (or consonant, vowel, consonant) words. They use common short letter sounds.

Complete Norman's words: last letters

Now Norman has lost the last letters in his words!
Can you help him to complete the words?
Write the missing last letter to finish each word.
Then write the whole word under the picture.

mat_

mat

ca_

ha_

ma_

ta_

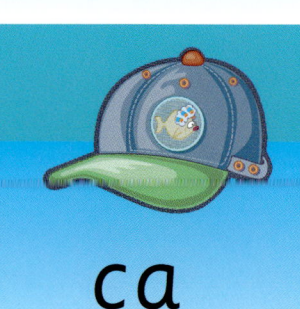

ca_

do_

lo_

le_

PARENTS' NOTE

These words are all simple CVC (or consonant, vowel, consonant) words. They use common short letter sounds.

Norman still can't find the last letters in his words!
Can you help him to complete the words?

bed
bed

re_

da_

ma_

ca_

pa_

ca_

ja_

PARENTS' NOTE
These words are all simple CVC (or consonant, vowel, consonant) words. They use common short letter sounds.

7

Complete Piska and Pod's words: CD
letters a and e

Help Piska and Pod to complete the words below.
Look at the picture.
Say the word and listen for the middle sound.
Write the letter **a** to finish the words.

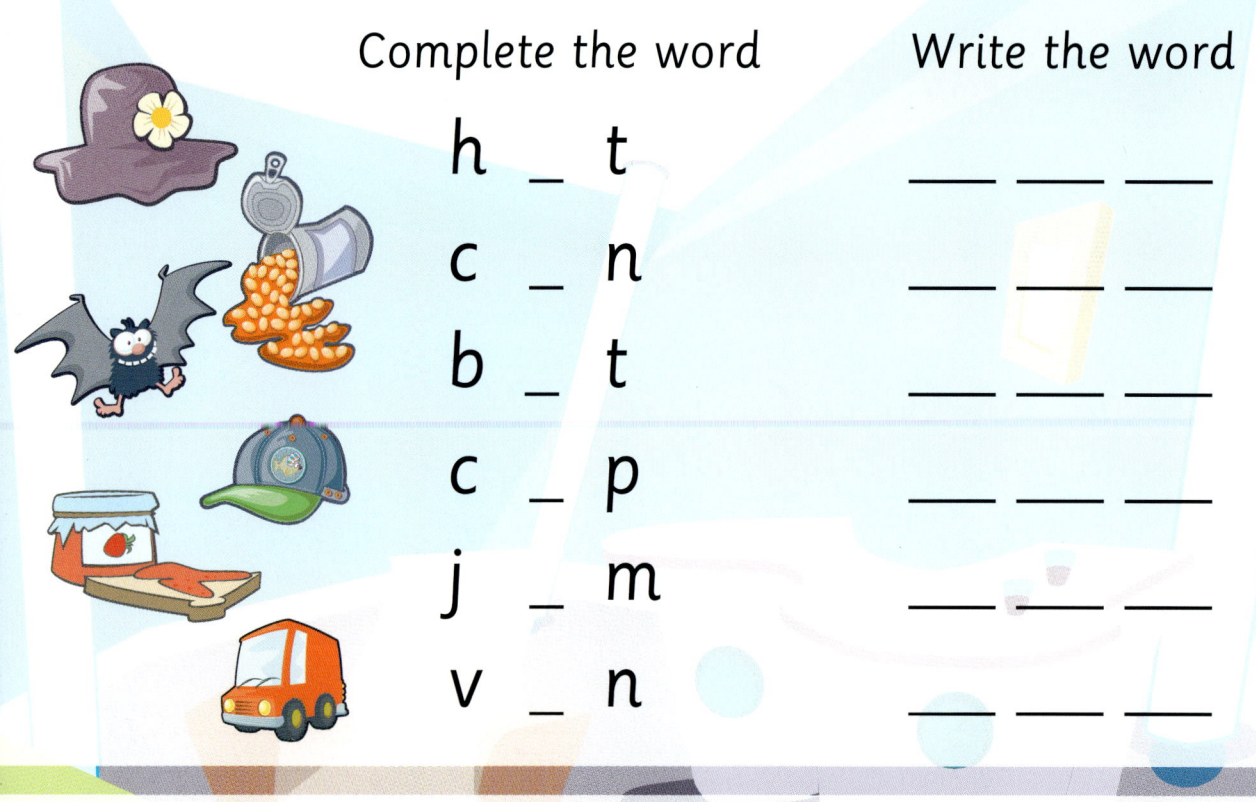

Complete the word   Write the word

h _ t   __ __ __

c _ n   __ __ __

b _ t   __ __ __

c _ p   __ __ __

j _ m   __ __ __

v _ n   __ __ __

Circle the pictures that rhyme with **hat**.

man    cat    cap    bat    bag

PARENTS' NOTE
Remember that the letters a and e may sound different when using different prefixes and suffixes.
For example snake and hat.

8

Help Piska and Pod to complete the words below.
This time you need the letter **e**.

Complete the word   Write the word

b _ d   ___ ___ ___

h _ n   ___ ___ ___

l _ g   ___ ___ ___

p _ n   ___ ___ ___

p _ g   ___ ___ ___

w _ b   ___ ___ ___

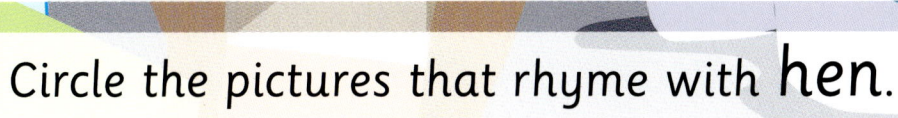

Circle the pictures that rhyme with **hen**.

web    leg   ten   bed    pen

PARENTS' NOTE
Try to find other words with a and e letters in the middle. Listen to the different sounds they can make.

9

Complete Piska and Pod's words: letters i and o

Help Piska and Pod to complete the words below.
Look at the picture.
Say the word and listen for the middle sound.
Write the letter **i** to finish the words.

Complete the word   Write the word

p _ g   ___ ___ ___

p _ n   ___ ___ ___

b _ g   ___ ___ ___

b _ b   ___ ___ ___

z _ p   ___ ___ ___

w _ g   ___ ___ ___

Circle the pictures that rhyme with **wig**.

pig    bin    bib    big    zip

PARENTS' NOTE
Remember that the letters i and o may sound different when using different prefixes and suffixes.
For example fire and pig.

10

Help Piska and Pod to complete the words below.
This time you need the letter **O**.

Complete the word   Write the word

b _ x   ___ ___ ___

l _ g   ___ ___ ___

p _ t   ___ ___ ___

c _ t   ___ ___ ___

f _ x   ___ ___ ___

d _ g   ___ ___ ___

Circle the pictures that rhyme with **hot**.

cot   dog   pot   fox   mop

PARENTS' NOTE
Try to find other words with i and o letters in the middle. Listen to the different sounds they can make.

Complete Piska and Pod's words: letter u

Help Piska and Pod to complete the words below.
Look at the picture.
Say the word and listen for the middle sound.
Write the letter u to finish the words.

Complete the word   Write the word

r _ g   __ __ __

b _ n   __ __ __

b _ g   __ __ __

s _ n   __ __ __

c _ p   __ __ __

m _ g   __ __ __

Circle the pictures that rhyme with rug.

bug    cup    sun    mug    hut

PARENTS' NOTE
Try to find other words with u in the middle. Listen to the different sounds they can make.

12

Complete the clamp's words: ch sound

The clamp is using the **ch** sound to complete these words. Some of the words begin with **ch** and some end with **ch**! Complete each word, then say it out loud.
Listen for the **ch** sound.
Now write the words on the lines.

Complete the word   Write the word

_ _ in   _ _ _ _

tor _ _   _ _ _ _ _

_ _ ip   _ _ _ _

ben _ _   _ _ _ _ _

_ _ icken   _ _ _ _ _ _ _

lun _ _   _ _ _ _ _

Circle the words that begin with the **ch** sound.

bench   chip   chin   torch   chimp

PARENTS' NOTE
Try to find other words with the ch sound. Listen to the different sounds they make at the beginning and end of words.

Complete the clamp's words: th sound

The clamp is using the **th** sound to complete these words. Some of the words begin with **th** and some end with **th**! Complete each word, then say it out loud. Listen for the **th** sound. Now write the words on the lines.

Complete the word   Write the word

_ _ ick   _ _ _ _ _

mo _ _   _ _ _ _

_ _ in   _ _ _ _

ba _ _   _ _ _ _

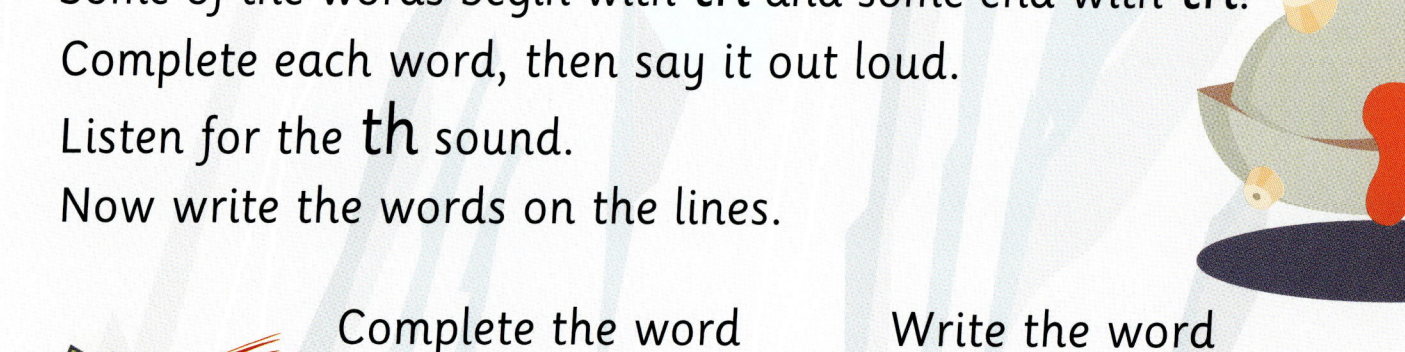

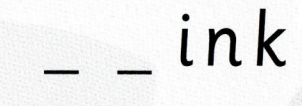

_ _ ink   _ _ _ _ _

pa _ _   _ _ _ _

Circle the words that end with the **th** sound.

bath   thin   moth   thick   path

PARENTS' NOTE

14 Try to find other words with the th sound. Listen to the different sounds they make at the beginning and end of words.

The clamp is using the **sh** sound to complete these words. Some of the words begin with **sh** and some end with **sh**!

Complete the word   Write the word

_ _ ip   _ _ _ _

bru _ _   _ _ _ _ _

_ _ ell   _ _ _ _ _

fi _ _   _ _ _ _

_ _ eep   _ _ _ _ _

di _ _   _ _ _ _

Circle the words that begin with the **sh** sound.

shell   fish   bush   ship   shop

PARENTS' NOTE
Try to find other words with the sh sound. Listen to the different sounds they make at the beginning and end of words.

Colours and numbers

The mullets have mixed up their paints.
Can you help them to match each colour word to the right pot?
The first one has been done for you.

Red   Yellow   Green   Blue   Black   White   Brown   Purple   Orange

Now say the colour names and
write the colour words on the lines below.

PARENTS' NOTE
If you have any paint pots at home, label them with stickers to reinforce colour word recognition.

Help the mullets to match up the numbers on the footballs to the right number words.

one • two • three • four • five • six • seven • eight • nine • ten

This is one of the mullets' favourite nursery rhymes. Can you complete the rhyme by filling in the number words?

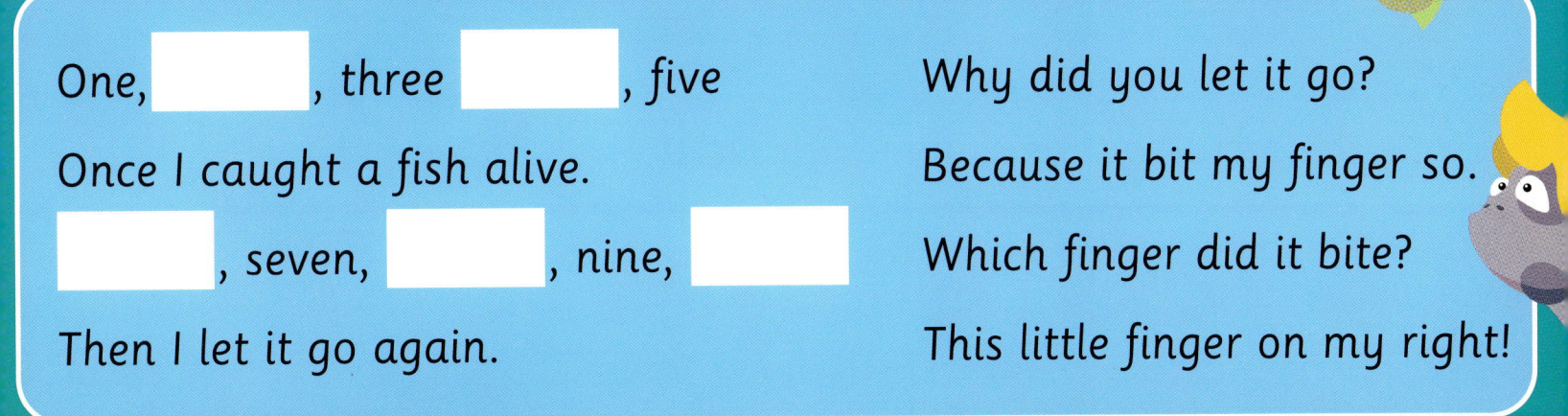

One, ____, three ____, five
Once I caught a fish alive.
____, seven, ____, nine, ____
Then I let it go again.

Why did you let it go?
Because it bit my finger so.
Which finger did it bite?
This little finger on my right!

PARENTS' NOTE
Use other number rhymes with your child to help to reinforce number word recognition.
Ten Green Bottles is a good example.

Complete Pike's words

Pike is using the ll sound to complete these words.
Can you help him?
Finish the words, then say each word out loud.

Listen for the ll sound.
Now write the words on the lines.

Complete the word   Write the word

hi _ _   _ _ _ _

ta _ _   _ _ _ _

ti _ _   _ _ _ _

we _ _   _ _ _ _

wa _ _   _ _ _ _

ba _ _   _ _ _ _

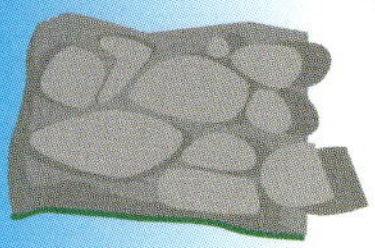

Circle the pictures that rhyme with **ball**.

bell 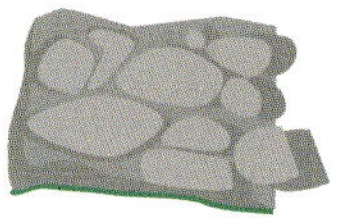   wall    bill    tall

PARENTS' NOTE
You can try this activity with other word endings: ff or ss are popular ones.

Pike is using the **ck** sound to complete these words. Can you help him?

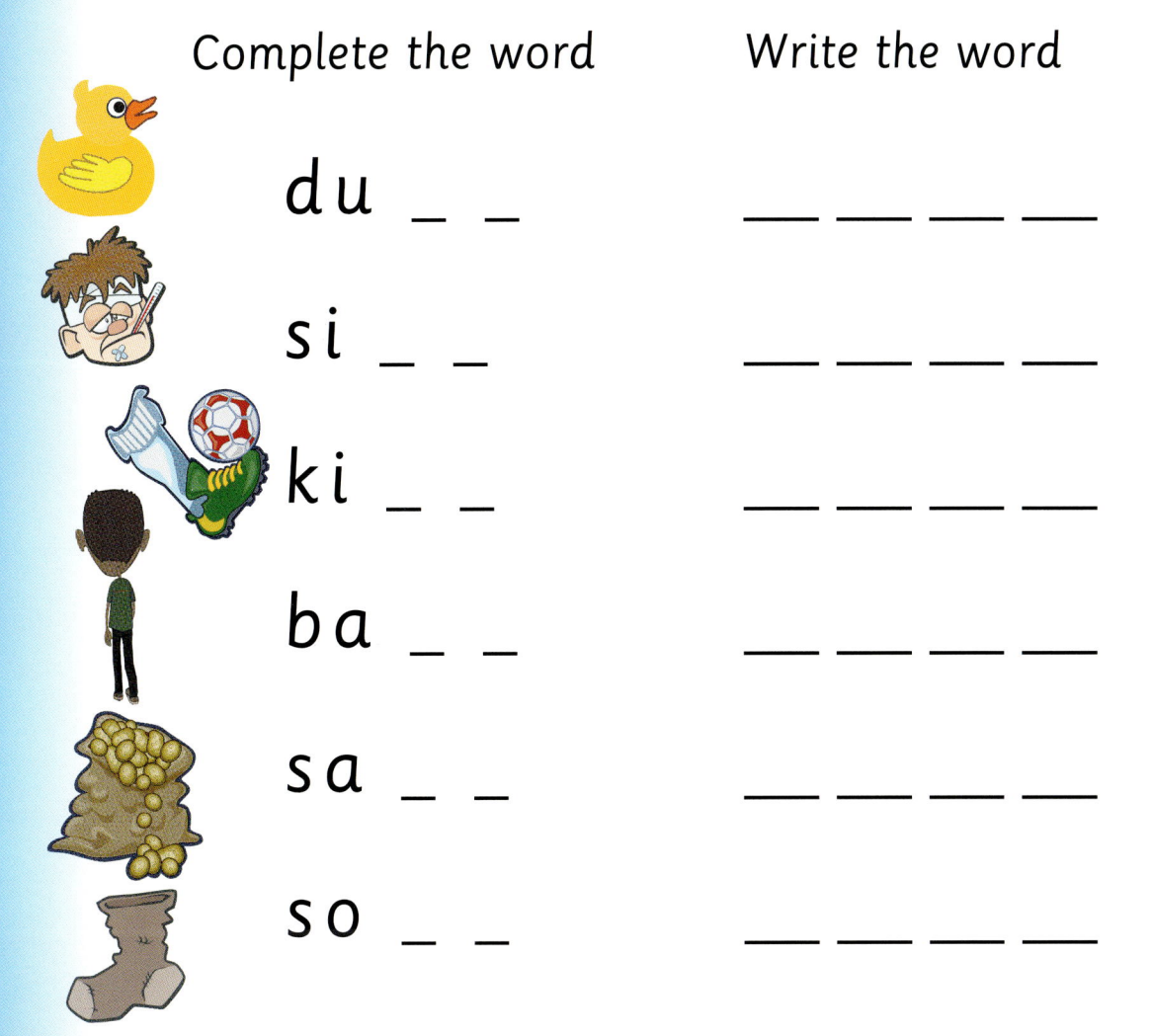

Complete the word   Write the word

du _ _   ____

si _ _   ____

ki _ _   ____

ba _ _   ____

sa _ _   ____

so _ _   ____

Circle the pictures that rhyme with **rock**.

kick   lock   duck   sock

PARENTS' NOTE
You can try this activity with other word endings: ff or ss are popular ones.

Complete Pike's words

Pike is using the **ng** sound to complete these words.
Can you help him?
Complete the words, then say each word out loud.

Listen for the **ng** sound.
Now write the words on the lines.

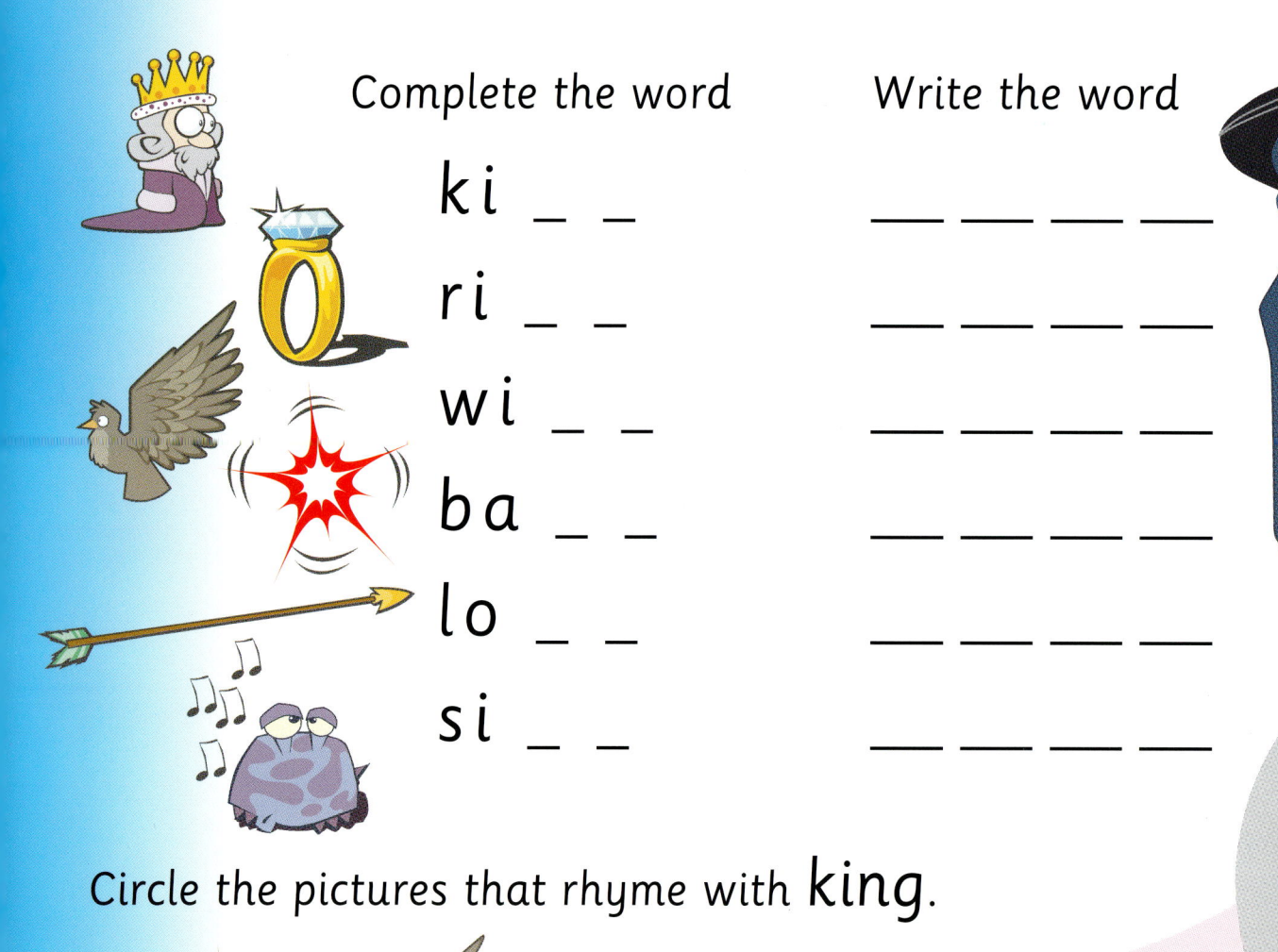

Complete the word   Write the word

ki _ _   _ _ _ _

ri _ _   _ _ _ _

wi _ _   _ _ _ _

ba _ _   _ _ _ _

lo _ _   _ _ _ _

si _ _   _ _ _ _

Circle the pictures that rhyme with **king**.

bang   wing   ring   long

PARENTS' NOTE
You can try this activity with other word endings: ff or ss are popular ones.

Sidney's word mix-up

a b c d e f g h i
j k l m n o p q r
s t u v w x y z

Sidney the Shark has mixed up his words!
Write the words in alphabetical order at the bottom of the page.
Use the alphabet at the top of the page to help you and
tick off each word as you write it.

Queen   Fox   Apple   Cat   Zoo   King   Hat
Sheep   Chip   Mug   Hand   Wall   Pan
Rug

_____   _____
_____   _____
_____   _____
_____   _____
_____   _____
_____   _____

PARENTS' NOTE
You can try this activity with family names, television characters or food to help children
to understand the order of the alphabet.

Capital letters

Names always start with a capital letter.

A a	B b	C c	D d	E e	F f	G g	H h
I i	J j	K k	L l	M m	N n	O o	P p
Q q	R r	S s	T t	U u	V v	W w	X x
Y y	Z z						

Write these names again,
starting each one with a capital letter.

jamie, tom, nick, usha, isobel,
katie, sidney and lin

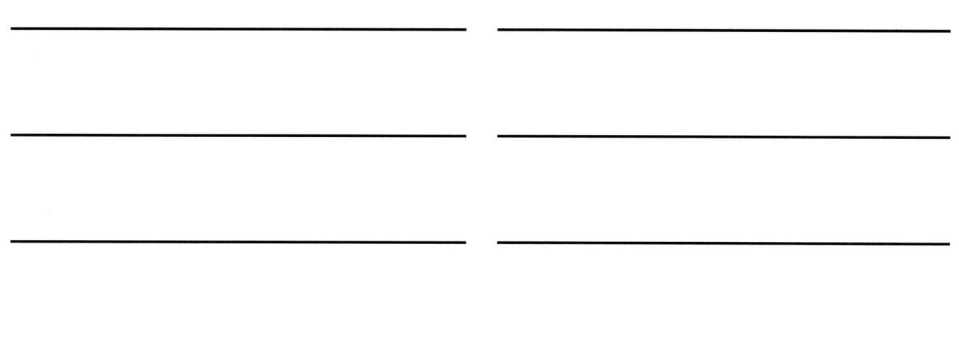

_____   _____

_____   _____

_____   _____

Now write your own name
starting with a capital letter.

_____

PARENTS' NOTE
Children might like to try this activity with their friends and classmates.

Draw a picture of yourself in this Spark Island frame.

My first name is..

My family name is...

I am .... years old.

I go to.. school.

My favourite colour is...

PARENTS' NOTE

Help your child to complete this page. It will show you how much they have learnt through the book.

23

How to use the CD-ROM

The CD-ROM is designed to provide your child with lots of exciting activities to help them to develop and practise core skills in English. You can also find a range of additional resources that you can print out and complete with your child. These are in the parents' section.

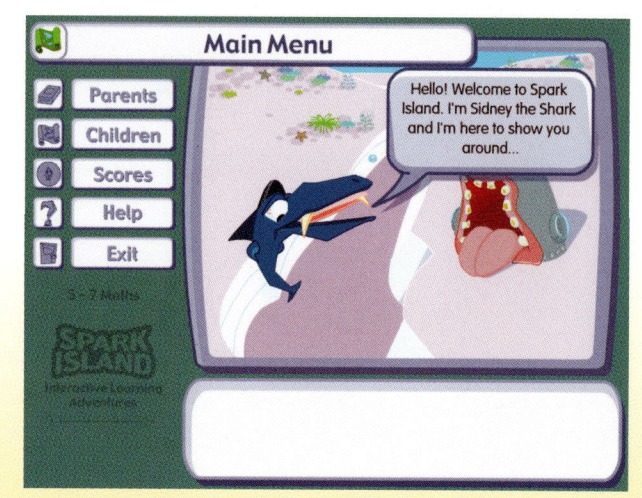

The Main Menu Screen

Parents
If you are a parent, click on the PARENTS button on the left hand side, where the activities are organised by topic. You can also find a whole load of extra things from activity sheets to pictures of your guide.

Children
If you are a child go straight to the CHILDREN button and find the activities on the colourful map.

Help
If you need help or further information about Spark Island, click on the HELP button.

Scores
To find out how you can score and save points, called megahops, click on the SCORES button.

Your guide to Spark Island

Have Fun!!

Sidney the Shark is your guide. He will help you to explore the CD-ROM and get the most out of Spark Island.

Installation instructions
This CD-ROM requires a Windows 95 (or above) PC or a Power Macintosh, with Internet Explorer or a similar browser installed. It does not require you to have any internet access. Your screen should be set to display in thousands of colours and at a resolution of 800 x 600 pixels or higher.

Technical Specifications
These CD-ROMs are designed to work on any reasonably modern computer, which will have at least the technical specifications given below.

PC
Microsoft Windows 95/NT 4.0 or higher with a web browser installed
Pentium-class processor 133Mhz or above with 32MB RAM
SVGA compatible graphics, 4x speed CD-ROM drive and a sound card
On a PC, the CD-ROM should launch automatically after it is inserted into the appropriate drive slot. If it does not, please select "Run" from the start menu and type d:\spark.exe, where d:\ is the letter designated to your CD-ROM drive.
Note that the program will not run without the CD-ROM in your CD drive.

Macintosh
System 8.x or above
PowerPC processor, 333 Mhz or greater
64MB memory
On a Macintosh, the CD-ROM should launch automatically after it is inserted into the appropriate drive slot. If it does not, please open the CD-ROM once it is displayed on your desktop and double-click on the Spark Island icon.
Note that the program will not run without the CD-ROM in your CD drive.

Discover secret treasure on Spark Island!

Come and explore at www.sparkisland.com/world3 – there are some free goodies waiting for you!

Spark Learning Limited, 28 Bruton Street, London W1J 6QW
Website: www.sparkisland.com

Published by BBC Educational Publishing, BBC Worldwide, 80 Wood Lane, London W12 0TT

Every effort has been made to trace copyright holders and obtain their permission for the use of copyright material.
The authors and publishers will gladly receive information enabling them to rectify any error or omission in subsequent editions.

All facts are correct at time of going to press.

Published 2002
Text © Spark Island

All rights reserved. No part of this publication may be reproduced, stored in a retrieval system, or transmitted,
in any form by any means, electronic, mechanical, photocopying, recording or otherwise, without the prior permission
of Spark Island.

British Library Cataloguing in Publication Data
A CIP record for this book is available from the British Library.

ISBN: 0 563 54561 5

Printed in Singapore.